Oxford

A little souvenir

CHRIS ANDREWS
PUBLICATIONS

Oxford

Introduction to Oxford

OXFORD may be seen as a seat of intellectual activity advancing the frontiers of knowledge, fostering the achievements of Roger Bacon, John Wycliffe, Robert Boyle, Edmund Halley, Howard Florey, and many others. Also it is the birthplace of the *Oxford English Dictionary*, the ultimate authority on the language, now in its up-to-date twenty-volume second edition.

OXFORD is the background of *Alice* and her wonderful world, of Thomas Hardy's *Jude the Obscure*, of Matthew Arnold's *Thyrsis*, of Dorothy Sayers' *Gaudy Night*, and of countless poems, novels, and fantasies. Shelley, sent down for professing atheism, Gerard Manley Hopkins, curate of St Aloysius R.C.Church; Michael Innes, a don behind a pseudonym; T.E. Lawrence, C.S. Lewis, J.R.R. Tolkein, Evelyn Waugh, John Betjeman, Nevill Coghill – they all owe something to Oxford, as do many others in less evident ways.

Merton College and Meadow Cottages in Christ Church Meadow   5

6   Duke Humfrey's Library

OXFORD gave a home to the Stuart Court – that 'centre of corruption and good taste' – when King Charles had his capital here from 1642 to 1646. At all times in history Oxford has nurtured statesmen, countless bishops and not a few archbishops, as well as pioneers, colonizers, and political leaders – including William Penn, James Oglethorpe, Cecil Rhodes, and more than twenty British Prime Ministers in the past two centuries. Oxford has seen the birth of religious movements inspired by men such as the Wesley brothers, and John Keble.

OXFORD may be seen materially as a concentration of handsome buildings dating

Wysteria in Jesus College   7

Oxford from the east

from as early as AD 1000, with an especially good representation of the 15th to the 18th centuries; here are fine examples of the work of William Orchard, Christopher Wren, Nicholas Hawksmoor, James Gibbs, and the Oxford amateurs Dean Henry Aldrich and Dr George Clarke. The great Victorian architects are prominent too; the Gilbert Scott family, William Butterfield, Basil Champneys, and Thomas G. Jackson.

OXFORD: the name may for some people conjure up tutorials and lectures attended when ostensibly, or earnestly, reading for a degree; or the tranquillity of riverside walks in the University Parks or Christ Church Meadow, and Commemoration Balls on warm summer nights. For boating enthusiasts Oxford can mean the finest reaches of the upper Thames or the most idyllic stretch of the lower Cherwell with a leisurely punt on a sunny day. Then there is Eights Week – dramatized for posterity in Max Beerbohm's *Zuleika Dobson*.

OXFORD has been lived in and loved or hated, but never ignored or forgotten, by a thousand years of Kings, Queens, philosophers, prelates, scientists, students, dons, and plain people.

12   Balliol College Garden Quad

Brasenose College Old Quad and the Radcliffe Square gateway   13

14   Christ Church, the largest Oxford College

16 Corpus Christi College, Front Quad and Pelican

Exeter College Fellows' Garden   17

18 Hertford College, inside the stair tower

Jesus College Inner Quad   19

20   Keble College and Oxford

22 Magdalen College, the New Buildings and spring flowers

Merton College, winters night   23

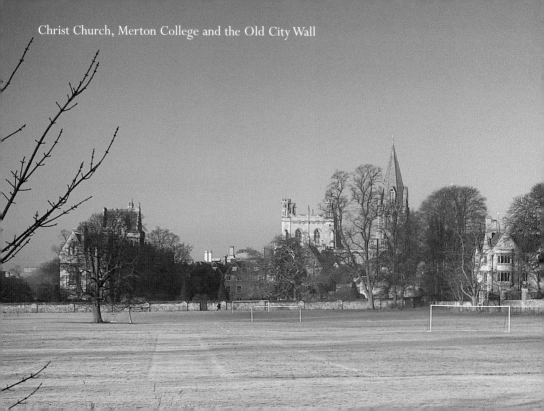
Christ Church, Merton College and the Old City Wall

26   New College Cloister

Nuffield College Spire with The Thames and The Oxford Canal   27

28   Oriel College Front Quad

Pembroke College, Chapel Quad and The Hall   29

30   Oxford from the north

The Queen's College, exterior of the library   31

32   St Anne's College

34   St Hilda's College and The Cherwell

St John's College, stone carvings on Canterbury Quad   35

36 Punting, an engaging Oxford pursuit practiced for centuries on The Cherwell and Isis

38 Trinity College, spring flowers in The Grove

University College, fan vaulting in Radcliffe Quad entrance   39

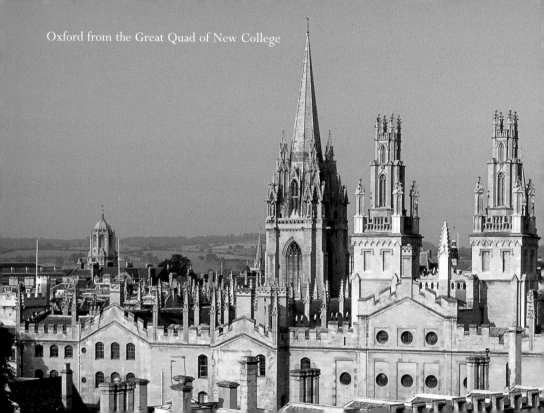

Oxford from the Great Quad of New College

42   Wadham College Fellows' garden

44   The University of Oxford Botanic Garden

46   The ceiling in Duke Humfrey's Library

48   The Radcliffe Camera

The Radcliffe Camera and St Mary's Church over The Bodleian Library roof   49

50   The University Church of St Mary The Virgin

The Sheldonian Theatre and The Clarendon Building   51

52   Oxfords "Bridge of Sighs" joining two parts of Hertford College

The Eagle and Child in St Giles, one of Oxford's older and better known pubs 53

54　The calm of The University Parks

56   The River Thames – or Isis, near Iffley

58   The annual summer rowing races, "Eights Week"

Early summer training when the river is quieter   59

60   Christ Church meadow flooded and frozen

62 Radcliffe Square, possibly the intellectual as well as literal centre of Oxford

First published 2005

by

Chris Andrews Publications 15 Curtis Yard North Hinksey Lane Oxford OX2 0NA

Telephone: +44(0)1865 723404 email: chris.andrews1@btclick.com Photos by Chris Andrews

ISBN 0 9540331 9 1 All material © Chris Andrews Publications

www.cap-ox.com

ACKNOWLEDGEMENT

Many thanks to the Colleges and University of Oxford for their encouragement and kind permission to show their many aspects. Christ Church by permission of the Governing Body of Christ Church, Oxford. The inclusion of a building or view in this work does not necessarily indicate a right of public access

Front Cover: Oxford from South Park
Title: Detail from the Bodleian ceiling.
Back cover: Encaenia in The Sheldonian Theatre